Forensic Crime Solvers

BLOOD EVIDENCE

By Barbara B. Rollins
and Michael Dahl

Consultant:
Catherine Knutson
Forensic Biologist
Minnesota Bureau of Criminal Apprehension
St. Paul, Minnesota

Capstone
press
Mankato, Minnesota

Edge Books are published by Capstone Press
151 Good Counsel Drive, P.O. Box 669, Mankato, Minnesota 56002
www.capstonepress.com

Library of Congress Cataloging-in-Publication Data
Rollins, Barbara B.
  Blood evidence / by Barbara Rollins and Michael Dahl.
    p. cm.—(Edge books. Forensic crime solvers)
  Summary: Describes how blood analysis is used to solve crimes, including the tests
performed by lab technicians on samples to determine blood type and other
characteristics, and finding, saving and interpreting blood evidence.
  Includes bibliographical references and index.
  ISBN 0-7368-2418-9 (hardcover)
  1. Criminal investigation—Juvenile literature. 2. Evidence, Criminal—Juvenile
literature. 3. Blood—Juvenile literature. [1. Criminal investigation. 2. Evidence, Criminal.
3. Blood. 4. Forensic sciences.] I. Dahl, Michael. II. Title. III. Edge books, forensic
crime solvers.
HV8073.8.R65 2004
363.25'62—dc22   2003013029

Editorial Credits

Carrie Braulick, editor; Juliette Peters, series designer; Jo Miller, photo researcher

Photo Credits

AP/Wide World Photos, Don Ryan, 15; Doug Mills, 10; Lefteris Pitarakis, 23;
    Reed Saxon, 28
Brand X Pictures, 22
Capstone Press/Gary Sundermeyer, 4, 6, 7, 8, 9
Corbis/Michael Prince, 14; Reuters NewMedia Inc., 1
Getty Images Inc./AFP/Gali Tibbon, 16; Mario Villafuerte, 24; Sean Gallup, 20
Index Stock Imagery/BSIP Agency, cover
Laboratory of Forensic Science/Herbert Leon MacDonell, 18, 19, 21
Minnesota Bureau of Criminal Apprehension, 12 (both)
PhotoDisc Inc., 29
Photo Researchers Inc./Dr. Jurgen Scriba, 26

1 2 3 4 5 6 09 08 07 06 05 04

Table of Contents

CHAPTER 1

Learn about:

• A murder scene
• Crime scene investigators
• Collecting blood evidence

The Body in the Shower

Paul Denby was the night security guard at the Hudson Tower apartments. His shoes squeaked as he checked the hallways on his hourly rounds. Denby stepped into the gym on the first floor. He looked down and saw a trail of dark red drops. Denby thought the drops might be blood.

The trail led to the back of the gym and into the men's locker room. There, a young man's dead body stretched across the shower's tiled floor. Denby reached for his cell phone and punched in 911.

Calling 911 alerts the police and emergency medical workers that their
◀ services are needed.

Collecting Evidence

Within minutes, police officers arrived. They stretched yellow tape around the area to keep evidence from being damaged. Soon, crime scene investigators (CSIs), a homicide detective, and a medical examiner (ME) arrived.

The CSIs took photos of the blood drops and studied them. One side of each drop formed a tail. The CSIs thought the blood had fallen from someone who had been running. They used cotton swabs to collect blood from the floor.

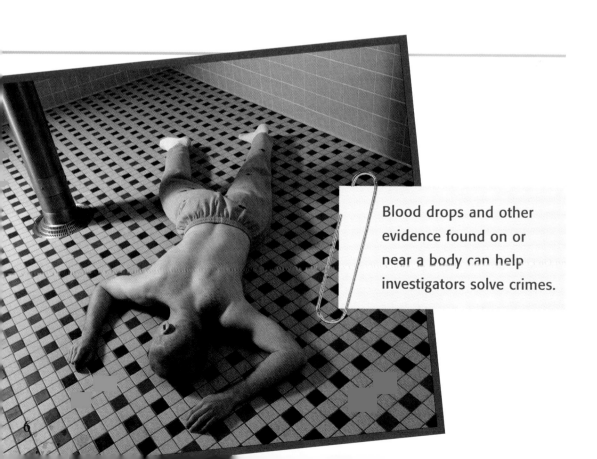

Blood drops and other evidence found on or near a body can help investigators solve crimes.

CSIs collect blood evidence from crime scenes.

The ME stepped toward the body. The dead man lay face down. He wore sweatpants and socks. The ME noticed spots of blood on the back of the man's pants. She turned the body over and saw thin, straight cuts in the man's chest. The victim had been stabbed eight times.

The detective and the CSIs searched the apartment building for more blood drops. The drops led them to a stairway. They found a small drop of blood at the top of the stairs leading to the sixth floor.

CSIs have equipment to help them locate blood on many surfaces, including carpeting.

Searching for More Clues

The blood evidence was sent to a police lab. A week later, the lab sent back a report. The trail of blood and the blood on the sweatpants had a different DNA profile than the victim's blood. The CSIs knew that it was from another person.

The homicide detective received search warrants to examine all of the sixth-floor apartments. The detective and the CSIs arrived at apartment 604. This apartment was rented by Henry Sheridan.

An Arrest

The CSIs sprayed luminol on the apartment's walls and floor. They turned off the lights. Large spots on the dining room's floor glowed blue-green. The CSIs knew that a large amount of blood had once been there.

The detective asked Sheridan where the blood came from. He had no answer. The detective took him to the police station for questioning. The lab later tested the blood in Sheridan's apartment. It had the same DNA profile as the blood leading away from the locker room and on the victim's pants. Sheridan was charged with murder.

Evidence collected by CSIs and good detective work helps investigators find suspects.

CHAPTER 2

Learn about:

- Phenolphthalein
- How CSIs use luminol
- Coomassie blue

Finding and Collecting Blood

Some blood is visible without a CSI's equipment. Other blood needs to be developed so people can see it. CSIs have chemicals and tools that can develop blood that is several years old. They also can develop blood that a criminal has tried to clean up.

Lights and Phenolphthalein

CSIs often use bright lights to find blood. They aim the lights at walls, floors, and ceilings. Many bloodstains that cannot be seen under normal lighting are clear under bright light.

If lights do show a stain, CSIs check if it is blood. They use a cotton swab to collect a small amount of the stain. They then spray or dab a chemical called phenolphthalein on the sample. The swab turns bright pink if blood is present.

Investigators examine each piece of
◄ evidence carefully.

Some bloodstains cannot be seen with the naked eye (left). Luminol makes the stains visible (right).

Luminol

CSIs may spray luminol on large areas if they think blood is present. Luminol reacts with a material in blood called hemoglobin. Stains glow blue-green or yellow-green if hemoglobin is present. CSIs can see the glowing stains in the dark. CSIs then do tests to make sure the luminol reacted with blood. Metal and some cleaning products also react with luminol.

Luminol can show blood on objects that appear to be clean. Hemoglobin often stays on fabric and other surfaces for months or years, even after many washings. Old bloodstains that react with luminol are brighter than new stains.

Other Chemicals

CSIs sometimes use a chemical called coomassie blue on tiled bathroom floors, sinks, and other smooth surfaces. A stain turns blue if blood is present.

CSIs can use leucocrystal violet on surfaces that absorb water, such as cardboard or carpet. If blood is present, the stain will turn dark purple or pink.

Blood Left Behind

Some crime scenes have blood, but no body. The amount of blood left behind at a crime scene can provide clues to investigators. A large amount of blood can mean that a person is weak or dead.

The human body contains about 6 quarts (5.7 liters) of blood. If a person loses more than 1 quart (.9 liter) of blood, blood pressure drops. Low blood pressure can cause a person to feel weak or dizzy. The person may faint. The loss of more than 3 quarts (2.8 liters) of blood is life threatening.

CSIs often use cotton swabs to collect blood from crime scenes.

Blood Collection and Storage

CSIs photograph bloodstains and collect the blood they find. CSIs scrape dried blood into paper containers. They use swabs or cloth to collect wet blood. These items are then dried and packed in paper.

CSIs store blood in coolers after they collect it. The temperature in the coolers is about 41 degrees Fahrenheit (5 degrees Celsius).

CHAPTER 3

Learn about:

- Shapes of blood drops
- Blood spatter
- Blood left by weapons

Bloodstain Patterns

Bloodstains form different types of patterns. Investigators study the patterns to help them solve crimes.

Blood Drops

The shape a blood drop forms on a surface depends on how far the drop fell. A drop falling a few inches leaves a thick, round stain. The drop has a smooth edge. A drop that falls more than 6 feet (1.8 meters) usually bounces. The blood drop forms a jagged edge, or crown.

Blood drops that travel quickly also form crowns. For example, a cut artery pumps out blood quickly. The drops form crowns when they land on a surface.

Each bloodstain can provide investigators
◄ with clues.

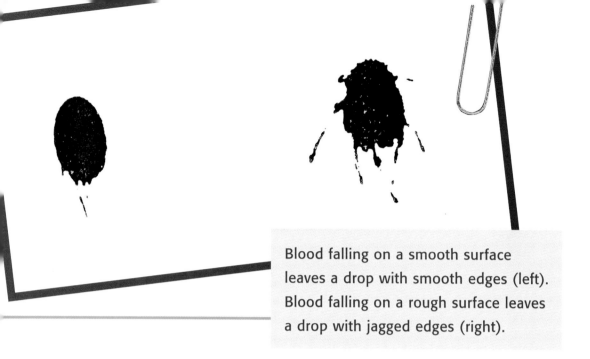

Blood falling on a smooth surface leaves a drop with smooth edges (left). Blood falling on a rough surface leaves a drop with jagged edges (right).

The shape of a blood drop also depends on where the blood lands. A drop landing on a smooth surface usually has a smooth, round edge. A blood drop falling on a rough surface usually forms a jagged edge.

Blood in Motion

Blood drops sometimes come from people who are moving. Blood from a moving person goes through the air at an angle. The angle affects the drop's shape when it hits a surface. Blood that falls at an angle has a narrow tail on one side. The tail points away from the direction of travel.

By studying blood drops, CSIs can learn about what happened at a crime scene. They may be able to tell which direction a bleeding person was moving. They also may be able to tell how heavily someone was bleeding. Closely spaced blood drops can show that a bleeding person was moving slowly or bleeding heavily. Blood drops spaced farther apart can mean a bleeding person was moving quickly or bleeding lightly.

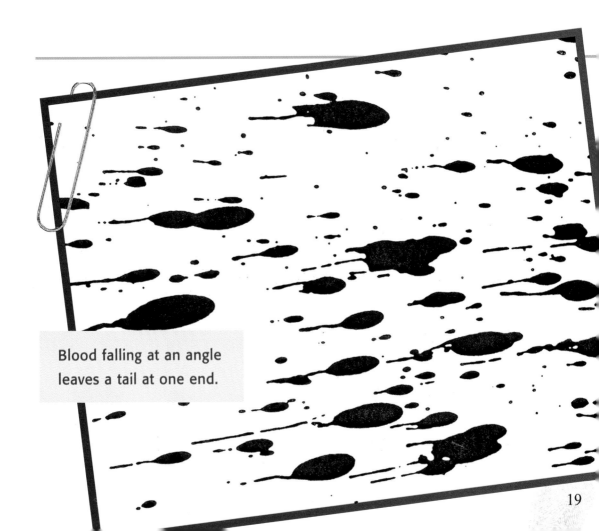

Blood falling at an angle leaves a tail at one end.

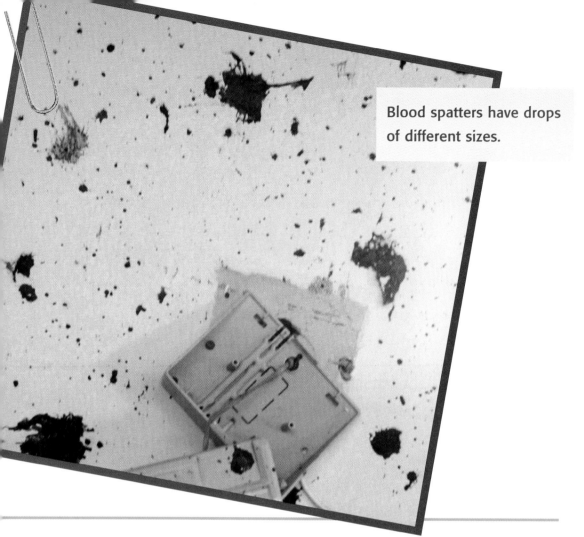

Blood spatters have drops of different sizes.

Blood Spatter

Spatters are blood drops of different sizes that form patterns. Cut arteries and bullet wounds can cause spatter.

A strike from an object also can cause blood spatter. A large object or an object moving quickly usually makes spatter with small drops. A small or slow-moving object usually makes spatter with large drops.

Blood spatters have a source. This area is called the point of convergence. A point of convergence helps investigators learn the location of a body during an attack. To find this point, investigators can enter blood spatter details into a computer program. The program shows where the blood source may have been.

Studying Bloodstains

The Bloodstain Evidence Institute in Corning, New York, teaches students how to examine bloodstain evidence. Students throw blood against walls, fling it from their hair, sneeze it through their noses, and spit it out of their mouths. They then study the patterns the blood forms.

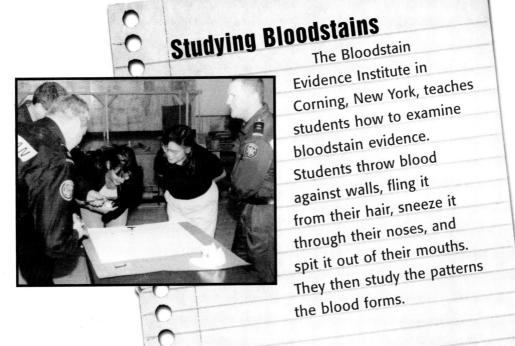

Types of Bloodstains

cast-off stain—a stain created when blood is thrown off an object in motion

expiratory blood—blood forced from the mouth, nose, or respiratory system

fly spot—a stain that a fly creates by resting in blood and landing in a different place

pattern transfer—a stain created when blood comes in contact with another surface; someone who steps in blood may cause a pattern transfer.

satellite spatter—a stain created when small blood drops move away from the main drop as it hits a surface

wipe—a stain created when an object moves through blood

Blood from Weapons

Many weapons leave behind certain types of bloodstain patterns. Bullet wounds often leave small, misty spatters. Spatter from an exit wound is called forward spatter. Spatter from an entrance wound is called backward spatter. Investigators can study gunshot spatter to learn the position of victims when they were shot. They also might be able to judge the position of the shooters.

Spatter from a stabbing or beating death may have cast-off patterns. These patterns are made when blood is thrown from a weapon. Several strikes to the same body part often make cast-off patterns. Investigators sometimes can guess what type of weapon was used in a crime by studying cast-off patterns. They also may be able to tell how many times or how hard a victim was hit.

Blood left on or by weapons can be important evidence.

CHAPTER 4

Learn about:

• DNA
• Types of blood
• Secretors

Blood in the Lab

CSIs send collected blood to a laboratory. Forensic scientists then test the blood. The test results can help investigators find or rule out suspects. They also can help investigators learn what happened at a crime scene.

DNA

In the late 1980s, forensic scientists started doing DNA tests. DNA gives people their individual characteristics. Only identical twins have the same DNA. Scientists can test blood, saliva, and other bodily fluids for DNA.

To perform DNA tests on blood, scientists add chemicals to a blood sample. The chemicals break open the cells and release DNA. The DNA then can be tested.

After a test, scientists study the pattern the DNA forms. A DNA match is made if a pattern from one sample matches another sample's pattern.

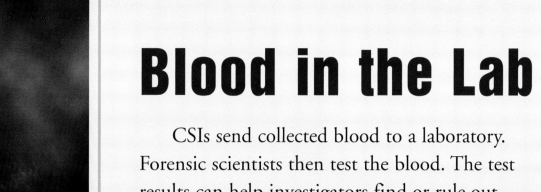

Forensic scientists carefully handle blood
◀ samples so DNA tests can be done on them.

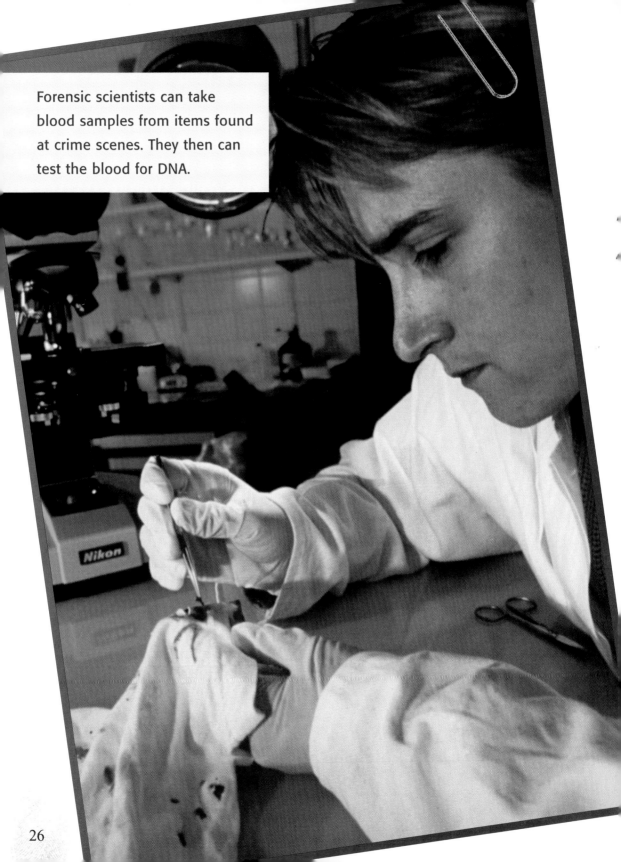

Forensic scientists can take blood samples from items found at crime scenes. They then can test the blood for DNA.

DNA tests that are done correctly are very accurate. Some tests have a 99 percent accuracy rate.

Scientists sometimes cannot perform DNA tests. There may not be enough DNA. Blood tests for DNA are only possible with white blood cells. Some blood samples do not have enough white blood cells. DNA also may be too damaged to test.

Blood Types

Each person has either *A*, *B*, *AB*, or *O* blood type. Before DNA testing was available, scientists tested blood to find out its type. Investigators used the test results to help them solve crimes. Today, scientists may still test for blood types when DNA testing is not possible. The test results can rule out or build evidence against a suspect.

Some people's blood type shows in their sweat, saliva, or tears. These people are called secretors. Scientists may test saliva on a cigarette butt or sweat on a sock to find a secretor's blood type. People who only show their blood type through blood testing are called nonsecretors.

Rhesus Factor

People who have a protein called the rhesus factor in their blood are Rh positive. Four out of every five people are Rh positive.

Scientists may test blood for the Rh factor if two blood spots are the same type. If the Rh factor is different, investigators know the blood came from two people.

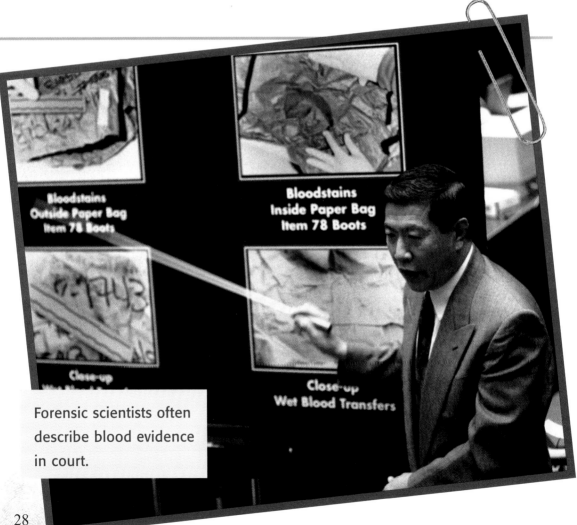

Bloodstains
Outside Paper Bag
Item 78 Boots

Bloodstains
Inside Paper Bag
Item 78 Boots

Close-up
Wet Blood Transfers

Close-up

Forensic scientists often describe blood evidence in court.

Using Blood Results

From the 1970s to the late 1980s, blood typing results were often used as evidence in court. Today, DNA test results are commonly used in court. In 1987, Tommy Lee Andrews became one of the first people in the United States found guilty of a crime based on DNA evidence.

DNA evidence has also helped free innocent people from prison. In 2001, Christopher Ochoa was freed from prison. A DNA sample taken from him did not match the DNA evidence from the crime scene. He had spent 12 years in prison for a murder he did not commit.

Blood evidence is one of forensic science's most powerful tools. Just a single drop of blood can help investigators solve a crime.

Glossary

blood spatter (BLUHD SPAT-ur)—a pattern of blood drops of various sizes

blood type (BLUHD TYPE)—one of four kinds of blood

crown (KRAUN)—a jagged edge on a blood drop

DNA (dee-en-AYE)—material in cells that gives people their individual characteristics; DNA stands for deoxyribonucleic acid.

hemoglobin (HEE-muh-gloh-bin)—a substance that gives blood its red color

luminol (LOO-muh-nahl)—a chemical that makes bloodstains glow blue-green or yellow-green

medical examiner (MED-uh-kuhl eg-ZAM-in-ur)—a public officer who examines bodies to find out cause of death

phenolphthalein (fee-nul-THA-lee-un)—a chemical CSIs use to find out if a sample is blood

rhesus factor (RHEE-sus FAK-tur)—a protein in the blood of most people

Read More

Fridell, Ron. *DNA Fingerprinting: The Ultimate Identity.* New York: Franklin Watts, 2001.

Friedlander, Mark P. Jr., and Terry M. Phillips. *When Objects Talk: Solving a Crime with Science.* Minneapolis: Lerner, 2001.

Owen, David. *Police Lab: How Forensic Science Tracks Down and Convicts Criminals.* Toronto: Firefly Books, 2002.

Platt, Richard. *Crime Scene: The Ultimate Guide to Forensic Science.* New York: DK Publishing, 2003.

Useful Addresses

Association of Certified Forensic Investigators of Canada
173 Homewood Avenue
Willowdale, ON M2M 1K4
Canada

National Center for Forensic Science
University of Central Florida
P.O. Box 162367
Orlando, FL 32816-2367

Internet Sites

FactHound offers a safe, fun way to find Internet sites related to this book. All of the sites on FactHound have been researched by our staff.

Here's how:

1. Visit *www.facthound.com*
2. Type in this special code **0736824189** for age-appropriate sites. Or enter a search word related to this book for a more general search.
3. Click on the **Fetch It** button.

FactHound will fetch the best sites for you!

Index